Monkeys

NorthWord Press
Chanhassen, Minnesota

DEDICATION
For Randy and Kat
     – D.D.

Photography © 2002: Anup Shah: cover, pp. 5, 21, 30-31, 42, 43, 44, back cover; Anup Shah/Dembinsky Photo Associates: p. 4; Alan Briere: pp. 7, 11; Shin Yoshino/Minden Pictures: pp. 8-9; Art Wolfe: pp. 12, 28, 35; Kevin Schafer/kevinschafer.com: p. 13; David Madison/Bruce Coleman, Inc.: p. 15; Norman Owen Tomalin/Bruce Coleman, Inc.: p. 16; Frans Lanting/Minden Pictures: p. 17; Alan & Sandy Carey: pp. 18, 23; Claus Meyer/Minden Pictures: p. 20; Erwin & Peggy Bauer: pp. 24, 41; Fritz Polking/Dembinsky Photo Associates: p. 27; Eric & David Hosking/Dembinsky Photo Associates: pp. 32-33; Stan Osolinski/Dembinsky Photo Associates: pp. 38-39.

Cover image: Douc langurs (*Pygathrix nemaeus*)
Illustrations by John F. McGee
Designed by Russell S. Kuepper
Edited by Judy Gitenstein

NorthWord Press
18705 Lake Drive East
Chanhassen, MN 55317
1-800-328-3895
www.northwordpress.com

Library of Congress Cataloging-in-Publication Data

Dennard, Deborah.
    Monkeys / Deborah Dennard ; illustrations by John McGee.
        p. cm. – (Our wild world series)
     Summary: Discusses the physical characteristics, behavior, habitat, and life cycle of monkeys.
    ISBN 1-55971-850-1 (hc.) – ISBN 1-55971-849-8 (soft)
    1. Monkeys—Juvenile literature. [1. Monkeys.] I. McGee, John F., ill. II. Title.
III. Series.

    QL737.P9 D44 2003
    599.8—dc21   200203262

Printed in Malaysia

10 9 8 7 6 5 4 3 2 1

Monkeys

Deborah Dennard
Illustrations by John F. McGee

NorthWord Press
Chanhassen, Minnesota

MONKEYS ARE THE CLOWNS and acrobats of the animal world. They amuse and delight people with their playful behavior and their expressive (ex-PRES-iv) faces. There is a lot more to monkeys than meets the eye, though. They are intelligent creatures, too.

Monkeys are primates (PRY-mates), just like apes and humans. They have 5 fingers on their hands and 5 toes on their feet. They have opposable (uh POE-zih-bull) thumbs on their hands. They have opposable big toes on their feet.

An opposable thumb can move across the hand to touch all the other fingers. An opposable big toe can touch all the other toes. Humans have opposable thumbs but not opposable big toes. Monkeys can grasp and hold things with their hands and their feet. They can pick up tiny things. They can pick up large things.

Proboscis monkeys are named for their unusually large noses. The word "proboscis" means nose.

Many monkeys are acrobatic climbers. These baby baboons are comfortable climbing right side up and upside down!

Primate heads are special, too. Their heads are large. Primates have big brains compared to the size of their bodies. Big brains are one of the factors that help to make primates smart. Most monkeys are full-grown in about 7 years. Humans are full-grown in about 18 years. The bigger the brain and the longer an animal is still growing and learning, the smarter it will be as an adult.

Tropical rain forests are the most common homes for monkeys. In rain forests they can find fruit and leaves to eat. They climb and jump and rest in the trees. Some monkeys even swing through the trees.

Not all kinds, or species (SPEE-sees), of monkeys live in rain forests, though. There are many different species of monkeys. They look different from each other. They eat different foods. They live in different places.

Monkeys
FUNFACT:

Monkeys and apes look a lot alike, but there is one big difference between them. Monkeys have tails and apes do not.

This pigtailed macaque uses his bright blue eyelids
to show off to other males and to females.

Some monkeys get all the water they need from the plants they eat.
These langurs are drinking deeply at the edge of a stream.

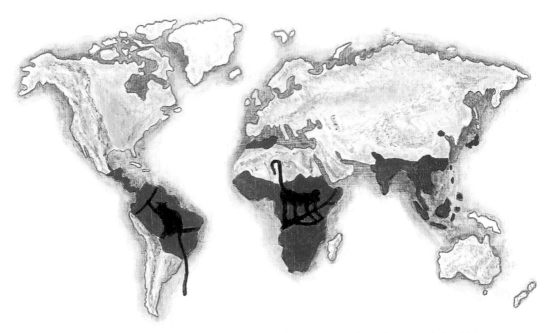

Red areas show where monkeys live in Asia and Africa (known as the Old World), as well as Central and South America (known as the New World).

Monkeys are divided into 2 large groups. One group lives in Central and South America. They are called New World monkeys. There are about 80 species of New World monkeys.

The second big group of monkeys lives in Africa, Asia, and in Europe on the Island of Gibraltar (ji-BRALL-ter). They are called Old World monkeys. There are about 75 species of Old World monkeys.

New World monkeys live only in the tropical forests of Central and South America. The smallest New World monkeys are called marmosets and tamarins. These tiny monkeys are about the size of a small squirrel but have the faces of monkeys. They have fine, silky hair. Some tamarins and marmosets have brightly colored fur. Others have manes like tiny lions, or crests like parrots, or long curving mustaches (mus-TASH-es).

Marmosets are among the smallest monkeys. They live in family groups of 2 to 4 and spend a lot of time grooming.

Tamarins and marmosets are the only monkeys that have claws. They have claws on all of their fingers and toes, except for their big toes. The claws help them to scamper up and down trees by digging into the tree bark. They leap like squirrels from tree to tree.

Tamarins eat fruits, flowers, flower nectar, small snails, lizards, and frogs. Marmosets eat fruit. They also eat tree gum or sap. Their bottom teeth act like special cutting tools to poke holes in tree bark. These holes let the sap, or gum, ooze out of the tree. The hungry marmosets lick up the sap. Tamarins can tell when other tamarins have been at a sap hole and move on to make their own sap holes.

Monkeys
FUNFACT:

Most monkeys have fingernails instead of claws.

Many tamarins and marmosets have showy patches of hair, crests, tails, and colors. These emperor tamarins sport some of the longest mustaches of all primates.

Black-tufted marmosets are always on alert to protect their small families.

Tamarins and marmosets live in many types of forests. They live in wet rain forests. They also live in dry forests where there are no leaves on the trees for about half of the year.

Other tamarins are found in brush lands. Brush lands are places where grasses, bushes, and shrubs grow tall, but where there are very few trees. Sometimes different species of tamarins live together and share the trees and plants. The emperor tamarin, with its large mustache, lives side by side with the colorful saddle-backed tamarin. The saddle-backed tamarin gets its name from the markings on its fur in the shape of a saddle. These two types of tamarins keep in touch in the dense rain forest with their high-pitched squeaking calls. Together they find the ripe fruits and defend their territories from other tamarins.

A capuchin monkey uses its opposable thumbs
as it unrolls a leaf to find a caterpillar to eat.

Capuchin (KAP-yeh-shen) monkeys are another species of New World monkeys. Capuchins are very intelligent and have unusually large brains for primates of their size. They eat fruit, like other New World monkeys. They also eat palm nuts that they crack open by banging on the trunks of trees.

Fruit and palm nuts alone do not provide enough protein, so capuchins also eat insects and snails. They even eat caterpillars. Capuchins find them by carefully unrolling the leaves where caterpillars may be hiding.

Capuchin monkeys are found from Honduras in Central America all the way down to the southern tip of Brazil in South America. Their territory is larger than that of any other New World monkey.

Capuchin monkeys use their tails for many different things like climbing and swinging, and for grabbing and carrying things like fruit and nuts. These strong and flexible tails are called prehensile (pre-HEN-sill) tails. A prehensile tail can be wrapped around a tree branch to help in climbing. A prehensile tail can even support a monkey's whole weight.

White faced capuchin monkeys are very intelligent.
Some have been trained to assist people with disabilities.

These three squirrel monkeys are scampering through well-marked treetop highways in their daily search for food.

Squirrel monkeys are small, graceful New World monkeys that live in groups of as many as 40. They scamper easily in the highest treetops. They often take the same paths through the tops of the trees in their daily search for food.

There are many monkeys larger and stronger than squirrel monkeys, but squirrel monkeys find strength in numbers. Much larger monkeys, like spider monkeys, will not challenge a group of squirrel monkeys for a tree rich with fruit. Squirrel monkeys also snatch up worms and caterpillars from the trees, eating them as they go.

Squirrel monkeys live in a variety of habitats: rain forests, dry forests, and palm forests. They even live near people and raid farms for food. In parts of South America they are called *maicero* (my-SAYR-o), or maize eater, because they steal corn from cornfields.

Spider monkeys are the largest of all of the New World monkeys. They can swing and climb through the trees with their arms and prehensile tails. Spider monkeys have much smaller thumbs than other monkeys. Instead of using thumbs, they use their long, hook-like fingers to hold on to branches. This is very unusual, because most primates have long opposable thumbs.

Monkeys
FUNFACT:

Only New World monkeys have prehensile tails. Old World monkeys do not have prehensile tails.

Some New World monkeys like this spider monkey have prehensile tails that act like an extra hand or foot.

Howler monkeys often make their loud calls
early in the morning or late in the afternoon.

Howler monkeys are some of the largest of the New World monkeys. The males can weigh up to 25 pounds (11 kilograms). There are 6 kinds of howler monkeys. Males of different kinds are different shades of black, brown, and rusty red. Females are smaller and not as colorful. Their fur is gray brown. Howler monkeys eat leaves instead of fruit. Leaves are tough and fibrous (FIE-brus), which means that they are stringy and hard to chew. Animals that eat leaves must have powerful grinding teeth for chewing the leaves.

Leaves have fewer nutrients (NEW-tree-ents) than fruit. Animals that eat leaves must also have special stomachs to get enough nutrients from the leaves. Leaves take a long time to digest. Howler monkeys must rest while their stomachs digest the leaves.

Howler monkeys have prehensile tails and strong arms. They do not swing through the trees, though. Instead, they climb through the treetops carefully, using their arms and legs and tails for balance.

Howler monkeys tend to stay in one part of their territory for a while before moving on to another part of their territory to look for food. While they are feeding in one small area, they are still protecting the rest of their territory with their hooting calls. The calls can carry for many miles. Because of their loud calls and slow movements, they are one of the easiest monkeys to see in the wild.

Monkeys
FUNFACT:

Howler monkeys are named for the roaring, howling noise
they make. They have a large voice box, or larynx (LAYR-inks),
that helps make their loud, howling call.

The uakari (OO-uh-car-ee) monkey might be the most unusual looking of the New World monkeys. They have bright red faces and heads. They have no hair on their faces. One kind of uakari has bright red hair. Another kind has long, fuzzy white hair.

Uakari monkeys live in the rain forest of the Amazon River basin. They eat leaves and fruit. They also eat the seeds of unripe fruit. This is an important part of their diet. Scientists know little about this species because they are very hard to find in the rain forest.

Monkeys
FUNFACT:

The only monkeys found in North America live in zoos.

The color of the uakari monkey's face varies from pink to bright red, depending on its mood.

Patas monkeys are excellent runners on the plains of Africa.
This baby holds on as its mother scampers along the ground.

On the other side of the world, there are monkeys in Africa and Asia. They are known as Old World monkeys. Some Old World monkeys live in trees, and some live on the ground.

Patas (PAH-tass) monkeys live on the ground. They are found in open savannahs (suh-VAN-uhs), also known as grasslands. Savannahs have very few trees and many different kinds of grasses. Patas monkeys sit up on their hind legs, or haunches (HAWNCH-iz), to scan the grasses of the savannah for danger. When trouble is near, they use their long legs to run away from predators (PRED-uh-torz). Predators are other animals, like cheetahs or lions, that might hunt them for food.

The largest group of Old World ground monkeys is the group of baboons. There are so many baboons because they eat a variety of food that can be found almost anywhere. The more kinds of food an animal can eat, the better chance it has for survival. Baboons eat fruit, seeds, plants, and meat. They dig underground for roots and bulbs. They sometimes hunt small animals. The males are fast and powerful runners and have very large, sharp, canine (KAY-nine) teeth. A group of hunting males can chase down a small antelope. Once they make their kill, they do not want to share, so they fight each other for the prize.

Another reason there are so many baboons is that they can live in many different places. Hamadryas (ha-ma-DRY-es) baboons live in near-desert areas of Ethiopia and Arabia. Gelada (je-LA-de) baboons live in the mountains of Ethiopia. In Tanzania, olive baboons live in the rain forest and on the open savannahs. In South Africa, chacma (CHOCK-ma) baboons live near water and even eat water lilies.

Baboons have arms that are about the same length as their legs. They walk on all fours through the grasslands. When they place weight on their hands, just their fingers touch the ground. They hold their palms up and away from the ground. Baboons have very flat feet that are not very useful for climbing trees.

Olive baboons often cuddle and groom each other in groups.
Grooming helps keep the animals clean and helps keep peace in the troop.

Another type of Old World monkey that lives on the ground is the mandrill. Mandrills are large and are often mistaken for baboons. They live on the ground like baboons. Unlike baboons, they live in thick forests in western Africa. Mandrills live in groups of as many as 700.

Monkeys
FUNFACT:

Mandrills are the largest monkeys in the world. Males can weigh up to 120 pounds (54 kilograms).

Male mandrills have brightly colored faces, which they use to show off to other males or to females.

The largest monkey: mandrill.
The smallest monkey: marmoset.

There are 19 species of macaques (ma-KACKS) living in many different places and habitats in the Old World. Some of them even live near people, so they are easy to spot.

Japanese snow macaques live near people. Food is placed by game wardens in parks and at the edges of the forests where the macaques live. This feeding allows the macaque groups to grow very large. Some macaque groups are as large as 1,000 monkeys!

Feeding by humans changes the natural way that the macaques get their food. This can cause problems in the troop because the macaques learn to fight for food rather than search for food. The strongest female and her family usually get first chance at the food provided by humans.

Monkeys
FUNFACT:

Japanese snow macaques live where winters are long and cold and snow is deep. In the winter, they find hot springs and take long, hot baths.

Japanese snow macaques have such thick, warm fur that they
can stand cold winter temperatures and even deep snowfalls.

Some langurs are called temple monkeys because they live near people,
even entering their temples or churches.

The Old World monkeys called colobines (COLL-uh-bines) are quite different from other Old World monkeys. Colobines lives in trees and eat leaves. Colobine monkeys have extra sharp molar teeth to shred the tough leaves into tiny pieces before swallowing.

Colobine monkeys in the Old World live much as howler monkeys in the New World do, eating leaves and slowly digesting them. Howler monkeys have special stomachs for digesting leaves, but colobines are even more unusual. They have 2 stomachs for doing the job.

The colobine monkeys of Asia are called leaf monkeys or langurs (long-GOORS). The Hindu people of India believe that hanuman langurs, also known as temple monkeys, are sacred (SAY-kred). This means they are special and may not be harmed, even if they steal crops from fields. Many of these monkeys live near people, often right in the towns. They are named after Hanuman, a monkey god in Hindu mythology. On certain days of the year these langurs are given food to eat in the Hindu temples. If one is accidentally killed, it is given a funeral and is mourned by the people.

Monkeys
FUNFACT:

Leaves do not have all of the minerals that colobine monkeys need, so to get more minerals, they eat dirt.

All monkeys, both Old World and New World, are social animals. This means they live in groups, or "troops," and like to interact (in-ter-AKT) with each other. Troop sizes can be as big as 1,000, like the Japanese macaques. With other species, troops can be as small as 4: a mother, a father, and their babies. This is very close in size to a human family. No matter the size, living in a troop keeps monkeys safe from predators.

Monkeys live in a variety of family structures (STRUCK-churs). Patas monkeys live in small groups of about 20, with several females and only 1 male. The male does not lead the group, even though he is twice the size of the females. The females lead the group, and the male follows along as a sort of bodyguard.

Red colobus monkeys are leaf-eating monkeys
that have 2 stomachs for digesting their tough, leafy food.

Olive baboons travel in large troops across the African plains.
They also enter forests and rain forests.

Some monkey troops are led by a group of females who stay together for their whole lives. Often female leaders have female babies that grow up to be the leaders of the next generation (jen-er-AY-shun).

Other types of monkeys are led by males. Olive baboon males are the strong leaders of their troops. Groups of male olive baboons form gangs that keep all of the other members in line. Within the troop there may be several gangs of males. The males in the strongest gangs are the ones who father the babies of the troop. They decide when the troop will move to find food and water and safety, and when it will stop to rest.

For other baboons, only the largest and strongest male becomes the leader. He is the only one to mate with the females. The leader gets first choice of food and is obeyed by all other members of the troop. Someday a younger male will challenge him. The leader of the troop will be the baboon that wins a bloody battle.

There are different ways in which monkeys and other primates communicate. Most monkeys communicate through sounds and actions.

Monkeys can be very noisy! Monkeys cannot use words like humans. Monkeys communicate by making different sounds. Squirrel monkeys keep in contact by making peeping noises when they cannot see each other in the dense rain forest. The farther apart they are, the more they peep. They twitter as a signal to move on. They make a low chucking noise when they are together to signal that all is well.

Marmosets communicate with trilling noises that sound like bird calls. Howler monkeys use pulsing, roaring calls that travel through the forest. Their throats balloon out as they howl, making the roar even louder and making the sound travel farther.

Vervet monkeys, an Old World species, have special alarm calls that tell other members of the troop when there is danger nearby.

The danger can be an eagle flying overhead, or a python slithering along the ground, or even a leopard in a tree. Scientists have studied vervet monkeys and have recorded their calls.

A large male baboon may smack his lips loudly or scream to show his strength. The scream, along with an open mouth to show huge canine teeth, is often enough to keep away intruders or to make a younger baboon behave.

Colobus (COLL-uh-bus) monkeys use a bellowing sound to keep their distance from other colobus monkeys. This helps them avoid getting too close to each other and fighting over food sources. They call to show where they are. As long as they hear each other but do not see each other, they are safe. Once two troops of colobus see each other, they stop roaring and make noise by shaking branches until one troop leaves.

Squirrel monkeys are so small and light that they can even climb out onto delicate palm fronds.

Monkeys communicate by sound. They also communicate with their faces. Monkeys have many facial expressions (ex-PRESH-uns) with meanings that other monkeys understand.

Monkeys often show an alert face with open eyes and lips that are slightly open. When they are ready to attack, monkeys open their eyes wide, and their mouths become a tiny slit.

When they are frightened, many monkeys open their eyes wide and open their mouths so wide that all of their teeth and their gums show. Monkeys show weakness by looking down with their eyes barely open. Their mouths are open enough to show their teeth. To a human, it looks like a small smile. A baby may beg with its mouth pushed forward in the shape of an "O."

Monkeys
FUNFACT:

Two monkeys greeting each other may show their pleasure by sticking out their tongues, opening their eyes wide, and making a sucking or kissing movement with their mouths.

Monkeys communicate many things with their faces:
a greeting (top left), begging (top right), fear (bottom left), and alertness (bottom right).

All members of a baboon troop want to smell, touch, and groom the new baby.

Touching is an important way to communicate. Monkeys spend a lot of time touching, or grooming, each other. Monkeys use their hands and sometimes their teeth to pick and comb through each other's hair. As they groom each other they remove dirt and insects, such as fleas. Grooming helps to keep the troop clean and healthy. Touch also can be very comforting, so grooming sends the message that all is well in the troop.

Monkeys groom each other in different ways. New World titi (ti-TEE) monkeys sit in pairs with their tails curled like a rope as they groom. Others, like some macaques, groom each other only at arm's length.

Grooming may show a monkey's "pecking order," or importance, in a troop. In some troops, the females groom the male leader for a long time. The male grooms back, but only for a short time. In this example, the male is higher up in the pecking order than the females.

Younger male monkeys may groom older, stronger males to show their respect for their leaders. Females may groom each other to show their friendliness. Males may groom females they hope will become their mates. And often all members of a troop groom babies and youngsters to show their interest and concern. Grooming helps the young monkeys learn the ways of the troop.

Monkeys
FUNFACT:

"Monkey see, monkey do" is an
old expression, but it is true.
Monkeys learn by looking and copying.

These Japanese snow macaques are warming themselves
in natural hot spring waters in the middle of winter.

Monkeys learn by copying the things they see other monkeys do.
This baby baboon is taking its first few steps away from its mother.

Babies are some of the most important members of a monkey troop. Baby monkeys and other young primates spend a long time in childhood. Babies depend on their parents and the other adults of the troop for almost everything. During these childhood years monkeys learn the many things they need to know to be an adult monkey.

Monkey babies are helpless when they are born. They depend on their mothers for everything, from getting milk to getting around. A tiny baby usually travels by holding onto its mother's belly or chest, often helped by the mother's comforting hand. A larger baby usually travels on its mother's back.

Marmosets are monkeys that do not depend on their mothers for very much. These tiny monkeys go to their mothers only for milk. The rest of the time their father carries them, grooms them, and cares for them.

In no time at all, the baby baboon has grown enough to play with other babies, away from the constant touch of its mother.

Squirrel monkey babies spend up to 2 weeks taking care of themselves. Their mothers do not seem to notice their babies at all for the first 10 days. The babies must hold on to their mothers by themselves with their tiny, strong hands and feet. They must find their mother's milk on their own. When the babies are close to 2 weeks old the mothers begin to pay attention to them and care for them.

Most primates take care of their babies as soon as they are born. No one is sure why squirrel monkeys do not.

Young monkeys, like young people, go through many stages of growth. They start by needing their parents for everything. As they grow, they become more and more independent. They are learning all the time, and then one day they will be able to survive on their own.

Monkeys like these langurs are dependent on the places where they live for their safety. Only there can they find the food and homes they need to survive.

The world of monkeys is a world of variety. No two species of monkeys are quite the same. No two monkeys are quite the same. Like people, they have their own personalities. Monkeys are intelligent animals that live in many places and in many ways. Their appearance can range from cute to frightening. Their behavior can be gentle or aggressive, playful or serious. What is true about all monkeys is they always surprise and amaze.

Monkeys need the protection (pro-TEK-shun) of people. Many monkeys are endangered (en-DANE-jurd) or threatened (THRET-end). Animals that are threatened may be in trouble if something is not done to help them right away. Animals that are endangered are already in trouble. Without protection, they could become extinct (ex-TINKD), or completely disappear.

The main reason that monkeys are in trouble is the loss of their territory. As people use the land where monkeys live, monkeys lose their homes. Without homes, they cannot live.

Can monkeys find safety in the world they share with people? Yes, with the help of caring people, monkeys and the places where they live can be saved.

One of the most important things to help save monkeys is to learn about them. Scientists are continuing their research so that people can better understand and learn from these fascinating animals. It is not just up to scientists, though. Anyone who loves nature and wildlife can learn about the primates with which we share our world.

Scientists are learning more about primates every day. There were 38 new species of monkeys found by scientists between 1990 and 2001. Most of those were found in the Amazon rain forest of Brazil. Two tiny species, found in 2001, are called the Bernhard's monkey and the Stephen's monkey.

No one knows for sure how many unknown species of monkeys are hiding in the rain forest. Unless those forests are saved, some species of monkeys could become extinct before anyone even knows they were there.

Internet Sites

You can find out more interesting information about monkeys and lots of other wildlife by visiting these Internet sites.

www.animaltime.net/primates/	Aye-Aye's Primate Primer
www.belizezoo.org/zoo/zoo/mammals/how/how1.html	The Belize Zoo
www.duke.edu/web/primate/	Duke University
www.enchantedlearning.com	Enchanted Learning.com
www.fonz.org/animals/af-primates.htm	Friends of the National Zoo
www.kidsplanet.org	Defenders of Wildlife
www.oaklandzoo.org/atoz/azvervet.html	Oakland Zoo
www.pbs.org/wnet/nature/gremlins/html/intro.html	PBS Online
www.primate.org	Primate Conservation, Inc.
www.rarespecies.org/pmarmo2.htm	Rare Species Conservatory Foundation
www.santabarbarazoo.org	Santa Barbara Zoological Gardens
www.scz.org/animals/b/baboon.html	Sedgwick County Zoo
www.sierrasafarizoo.com/animals/patasmonkey.htm	Sierra Safari Zoo
http://wcs.org/7823	Wildlife Conservation Society

Index

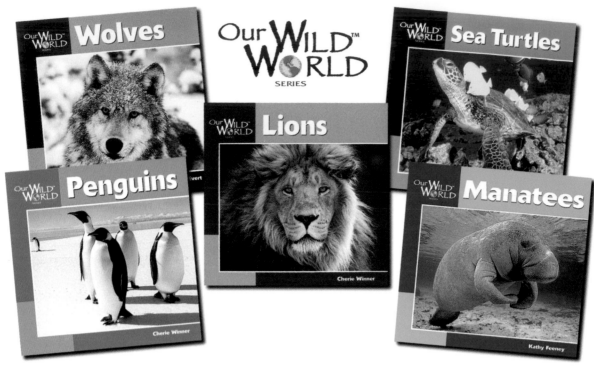

Titles available in the Our Wild World Series:

BISON
ISBN 1-55971-775-0
BLACK BEARS
ISBN 1-55971-742-4
CARIBOU
ISBN 1-55971-812-9
CHIMPANZEES
ISBN 1-55971-845-5
COUGARS
ISBN 1-55971-788-2
DOLPHINS
ISBN 1-55971-776-9
EAGLES
ISBN 1-55971-777-7
GORILLAS
ISBN 1-55971-843-9

LEOPARDS
ISBN 1-55971-796-3
LIONS
ISBN 1-55971-787-4
MANATEES
ISBN 1-55971-778-5
MONKEYS
ISBN 1-55971-849-8
MOOSE
ISBN 1-55971-744-0
ORANGUTANS
ISBN 1-55971-847-1
PENGUINS
ISBN 1-55971-810-2
POLAR BEARS
ISBN 1-55971-828-5

SEA TURTLES
ISBN 1-55971-746-7
SEALS
ISBN 1-55971-826-9
SHARKS
ISBN 1-55971-779-3
TIGERS
ISBN 1-55971-797-1
WHALES
ISBN 1-55971-780-7
WHITETAIL DEER
ISBN 1-55971-743-2
WOLVES
ISBN 1-55971-748-3

See your nearest bookseller, or order by phone 1-800-328-3895

NORTHWORD PRESS
Chanhassen, Minnesota